On Holy Ground

On Holy Ground

You and Your Faith Story

I. ROSS BARTLETT

RESOURCE *Publications* • Eugene, Oregon

ON HOLY GROUND
You and Your Faith Story

Resource Publications
An Imprint of Wipf and Stock Publishers
199 W. 8th Ave., Suite 3
Eugene, OR 97401

www.wipfandstock.com

PAPERBACK ISBN: 978-1-5326-1572-6
HARDCOVER ISBN: 978-1-5326-1574-0
EBOOK ISBN: 978-1-5326-1573-3

Manufactured in the U.S.A.   JANUARY 27, 2017

Contents

Tables and Diagrams

Preface

A book about sharing faith stories is clearly the product of the insights of many. I am grateful to those who helped in a process which, for me, has been going on for a number of decades. I first became interested in this topic when, as a newly-minted seminary graduate, I was invited to be part of a denominational task group engaging the United Church of Canada in the project *Confessing Our Faith*. My interest has continued as I have wrestled with the very poor "fit" of many evangelism models with my church's personality and yet the discomfort many of my parishioners feel in speaking about their very real faith. This book is an attempt to go a slightly different direction in meeting that challenge.

Thanks are due to the following who gave specific permission for the gathering of materials originally published elsewhere. Given that resources are often shared in different forms and experienced and recalled in different ways, I recognize that the sources cited here may not be the first place of publication. So I would appreciate any information regarding more complete acknowledgement

- The Rev Dr Hallett Llewellyn, Secretary, Theology, Faith and Ecumenism, United Church of Canada;

- Ms Marilyn Harrison, Chairperson, Confessing our Faith Project, United Church of Canada;

- Ms Betty Smythe, Resource Consultant, *Exchange Magazine*.

Thanks are also due to Knox United Church, Lower Sackville, Nova Scotia for agreeing to a sabbatical during which most of the writing took place; to the Collegeville Ecumenical Institute, Collegeville, Minnesota for a wonderfully rich and rewarding space in which to reflect and write, and the Board of Governors, Pine Hill Divinity Hall, Halifax, Nova Scotia, for generous financial support.

The finished product benefitted immensely from reading and suggestions from several people: Ruth Noble, Catherine MacDonald, Phil Kennedy. Rob Fennell. Copy-editing was done by Erin Labrie. Tracey Miller, my administrative colleague, works to keep me on track. Profound thanks to John Parkhurst for permission to reproduce his evocative photographs throughout the text.

Special thanks always to Heather, whose encouragement keeps me probing the mystery and wonder of the story.

Halifax, NS
Advent 2016

Introduction

You the Pilgrim

Off the southwest coast of Scotland lies the rugged island of Iona. Sometime in the sixth century an Irish monk named Columba arrived there, beginning the process of bringing Christianity to that part of the British Isles. From there, scores of missionaries went forth to carry the faith into present-day Scotland and England. If you go to Iona today, you can stay at the refurbished abbey. Once a week visitors are invited to go on the pilgrimage, a walk of about eight or nine miles as the crow flies, to places of spiritual and historic importance. But who among us is a crow? It's a lovely walk on a nice day, but the last time I did the pilgrimage it was raining and cold—oh my it was cold! You learn things on a journey like that. For instance, there are times when you can safely turn back but if you pass those you must press on to the next point before the option arises again. Or that a pilgrimage is not just about the destination but the fellowship along the way. Perhaps the only thing that keeps you going is the fact that you've set yourself a task and you're determined to complete it. But, most important, you learn the value of companions: support to one another and the entire community.

My companions were people I had never met before that day. There was Malcolm, an oil dealer and geophysicist, who had just committed his life to ministry; Melissa, a teenager seeking direction for her life; Tomas, Sean, Liz, Betty, and Andrew, a staff team from a social justice agency in Belfast, seeking refreshment and renewal for their work of healing and reconciliation; Kitty, in her wheelchair, for whom the pilgrimage was so important that this group (who had been strangers twenty-four hours previous) took turns carrying her up and down rain-slicked hills; Alec, who had been on the pilgrimage before and had to be carried off by emergency responders and now, at age seventy-six, was determined to complete it. A strange lot of people, so different in background, ability and expectation with little in common in the ordinary way of considering the world. Not the companions I might have chosen but the ones given by God.

There is a simple premise underlying this brief book: you have a faith story that is important. You may never have been told that before. Nonetheless, it is true. There's a good chance that you've never been shown how to tell that story. You may feel intimidated or turned off by folk who "share faith" in easy, self-confident, and sometimes glib ways. Perhaps you imagine that your life is not important enough or dramatic enough to be the basis for a story anyone cares about. Forgive my bluntness, but you're wrong. Your silence does no one any good—not you, or your neighbour or friend, or God.[1] It's not true to who you are. As the ancient Christian wrote: "Always be prepared to give an answer to everyone who asks you to give a reason for the hope that is in you—but do so with gentleness and respect." (1 Peter 3:15–16). The purpose of this book is fourfold:

1. To help you clarify your faith and express that faith;

2. To think about the language you can use to express your faith;

3. To think about the everyday reality of your relationship to God and Jesus Christ;

4. To consider ways in which you could feel more comfortable and confident in expressing these deep truths in conversation with others.

I promise you that there are some things this book *will not do*:

1. It will not presume to give you one right answer for your deep questions—those answers are for you to find;

2. It will not give you a sure-fire formula to convert your unbelieving friends or coworkers—no technique can replace your honest and respectful relationships;

3. It will not bolster the assumption that anyone who differs from you is wrong or, even worse, eternally condemned. It

---

1. The term "God" is one of those words that may lead to more confusion than clarity, and a lot less light than heat! Part of the problem is that most people who use the word God have certain meanings associated with it. But my meanings may well be different than yours. Because of a whole host of influences "God" may be a positive term to you and a negative one to someone else. When I say "God" you might think of an old, white male figure sitting on a cloud throwing thunderbolts or pulling strings—which is about as far away as anything could be from what I have in mind! So it might be safer to avoid all use of the word—except in a book about our faith stories than doesn't work. So when you read "God" here—unless I clarify it in some way—I invite you to think of it in the most positive of ways. You might want to substitute a term like "the Holy" or "the Ground of All Being" or "Eternal Truth" or whatever term you prefer for that which is beyond our knowing and control and yet is involved (in ways we can never fully encompass or describe) in all Creation—including you and me.

may even open you to the joyful risk of learning from others because I believe that the Spirit can speak to us from many places—including the most unexpected.

The underlying metaphor for this book is the *pilgrimage*. That may sound like a churchy word that has very little to do with the day to day of paying the bills, going to work, tending relationships, and experiencing both joy and heartache. We may associate the term with journeys to special places or famous journeys. The *Camino de Santiago* in Spain is perhaps the most famous spiritual walk, but there is actually an International Symposium for Pilgrimage Studies that gathers scholars and walkers from around the world who both study and participate in this form of devotional activity.[2] Cathedrals at Lourdes and Chartres (to name only two) are famous for the pilgrims they draw. For Moslems, the great pilgrimage is the *haj*—a journey to the birthplace of the Prophet which each devout Moslem, whose circumstances allow, is expected to undertake once in a lifetime. In some traditional societies there is the practice of the "spirit quest". However, I would extend the concept of pilgrimage to other places to which people flock—such as Graceland or Green Gables. If you have ever been there you've seen the busloads of awestruck travellers, filled with wonder at actually being on this special turf. Sometimes there are family pilgrimages, where the next generation is taken "back home" to see the roots from which the family sprang. There can also be mental pilgrimages: those times you may recall when you spent five minutes labouring over a single sentence in a book and you'd swear you could feel your head expanding as the new knowledge moved in. Then there are situational pilgrimages when we volunteer to go outside our comfort zone and help in a new space: perhaps in another country or more locally in a soup kitchen, shelter or prison. From that very brief list it is probably obvious that pilgrimage can take many forms.

2. See: http://www.wm.edu/sites/pilgrimage/annualsymposium/ accessed March 30, 2016.

From time to time in the book you'll run across conversation boxes. They are an invitation to pause and reflect—and perhaps jot some notes or even more in a journal. A journal is a great tool to take on any sort of pilgrimage.

All travelers are not the same. Who are you? A vagabond has no home; a fugitive is running away from home; a stranger is someone who is away from their home. A pilgrim is on her or his way back home, although that journey to their true location might take them to some unfamiliar places along the way. So, who are you? The pilgrim recognizes that the direction is not always clear and we may need to try a road for a time before we are convinced that it's the right one. We need to read, and talk, and watch, and listen widely before we find our proper location—which is merely the starting spot for the next stage of travel.

Since we're going to be travelling together for a bit you might want to know a bit about your companion. If not, you can skip this section without hurting my feelings in the least. What are the factors important in my journey at the present? I am married to a wonderful wife who works in the health care field. I am the proud father of two young adult daughters who continue to teach me about the wonders of the creation even as they did when they were younger. I grew up in the church and after spending some years away from it, I came back, was trained, and ordained. The focus of my working life is an active suburban congregation where I learn new things each day about the infinite ways in which people can experience and appreciate the presence of God and the number of ways in which people can feel hurt, abandoned, or betrayed by God or their faith community. I am convinced, because of a number of life experiences, that there is a God who wishes to be in a relationship with you and me; a relationship that involves communication. That relationship asks of us the time and attention to look and to listen. Listen in events as rare as a sunrise on a mountain lake or the tragic death of a close friend. Through ordinary events such as walking to the car in the morning or picking up the kids from daycare. God doesn't set up those things, the good and bad, the tragic and triumphant, but God will communicate with us through them. But the listening is something we have to do for ourselves. There is very little that ticks me off more than someone trying to interpret authoritatively the events in someone else's life! The best we can do is offer suggestions, gleaned from our own experiences of the journey, and share those humbly and gently. If anything this book is an invitation to listen to your life. "See it for the fathomless mystery that it is. In the boredom and pain of it no less than in the excitement and gladness of it, touch, taste, smell, hear, speak your way into the holy and hidden heart of your life because, in the last analysis, all the moments are key moments and life itself is grace." [3]

Years ago an older, rural church leader said something to me I've never forgotten.

> I imagine the last time anyone asked me about my faith was back in confirmation class. Now and then my kids asked questions but I never thought my answers were very good. After all, what do I know? The minister has all that training. I don't have the words. Sometimes I don't even understand what I read in our denominational magazine. I guess I've got a faith but no one has ever asked me about it.

That's a depressingly familiar story. Maybe it's yours. Jesus of Nazareth once asked: "Who do people say I am?" His followers gave him a variety of answers. That's a divisive question because you can count up the number of people who give a particular response and decide who's right and wrong. Then he asked: "Who do you say I am?"[4] That's a confession question because no amount of wriggling avoids a personal answer. This book arises from the conviction that we need to move from reciting others' answers to framing our own.

In this book I use the words *faith*, *spirituality* and *religion* in fairly specific ways. I'm not claiming they are the only ways or the right ways! But if we're going to understand one another it helps to be clear.

Faith: trust or confidence in something or someone;

3. Buechner, Listening to Your Life, 2.
4. Matthew 16:13 and Mark 8:27.

Religion: a system of beliefs that is codified or coordinated and expressed through communities of people such as churches, synagogues, mosques and so on;

Spirituality: relating to the human spirit or soul, usually in the form of convictions about life and truth and so on.

Did you notice what isn't there? *Belief.* The problem with the term belief—although it's a perfectly good word—is that many modern folks associate it with particular types of "head" knowledge. People are sometimes said to believe if they can recite specific passages, or agree to certain propositions, or sign onto a particular statement. The problem with belief is that it is possible for us to do all of those things and not place our trust in them.[5] On this pilgrimage we're interested in faith, because that's the story in you that has the potential to change life all around you.

One final thought: just as on that pilgrimage on Iona that began this chapter, so too in most of our pilgrimages (whatever form they take) companions are a true gift. Someone who can hear our new insights, share our fears and our joys, and help us up if we stumble or fall can make the journey much richer. So, as we start, I encourage you to think of someone else—or a group of people—to share this pilgrimage.

---

5. Five frogs were sitting on a log. Four decided to jump off. How many frogs were sitting on the log? Answer: Five. Deciding to do something and doing it are very different! Taken from the signature line of an acquaintance's email.

What is the most important thing to you about your faith? Can you make a list of all the things/people you have faith in? (I hope it's a long list!)

At times of trouble, doubt or difficulty, what story, saying or song comes to mind to give you hope?

What do you know about the faith of a person close to you? (It could be a family member, coworker or friend)

When was the last time you remembering sharing faith with a friend? How did that go?

Chapter 1

You the Theologian

As I sit down to write this chapter the news is filled with accounts of another terrorist attack on a European capital. Once more there are the growing lists of casualties—men, women and children—who were going about their own lives, joyful or sorrowful, purposeful or mundane, lonely or bathed in community. Once again the talking heads are doing their best to explain the reasons for the carnage. Once again the politicians are weighing in—some to urge calm, some to leverage the events into greater support for their policies of fear towards the unnamed but threatening and mysterious "other". Once again some folk will use the events as evidence, on the one hand, that there is no God or, on the other hand, that this is what happens when people believe in God. Once again, ordinary people of faith struggle to make sense of human heartbreak in a world view that includes God.

Consider your reaction to the following phrases and sentences:

- " . . . the end of all our exploring will be to arrive, where we started, and know the place, for the first time." T. S. Eliot, "Little Gidding".

- "The gospel never comes to us hanging in the air. The gospel comes to us in the situation in which we live, struggle, and respond to God. We have to apply the power of this word to the situation in which we live." South African church leader, Allan Boesak, addressing the World Council of Churches, 1993.

- "Unless we live our lives into our text, we leave God out." West German theologian, Dorothee Soelle. before the World Council of Churches in Vancouver, 1993.

- "Theology is the reflection of believers on what is God's purpose for us in and through Jesus. The church alone is not the source of theology, but it also comes from (i) contemporary human experience; and, (ii) tradition and experience. These must be in mutually critical correlation. Neither superior nor inferior, they must work together. Faith enlightens life while life enlightens faith." European theologian Edward Schillebeeckx.

- "In the beginning was the Word and the Word was with God . . . and the Word became flesh and dwelt among us." John 1:1

Each of these excerpts speaks about what theology is. What strikes me about them is the degree to which they move theology from something that is "out there"—done by professionals in particular settings—and into the place where you and I live each day. Directly or indirectly they speak of the importance of life in the process of theology. And it is a process; a back and forth or journey, rather than an arrival once and for all. In the journey of this *book you and I are engaged in theology—trying to speak plainly about the realities we have already grasped (or been grasped by) through faith.*

T he roots of the word *theology* are found in two Greek words: *theos* (God) and *logos* (word). Theology is the activity of speaking about God—who God is, God's actions in creation, and God's relationships with people. We might think of it as a conversation along the way as we go on our pilgrimage. Certainly, there are people—called theologians—who often bring special skills and study to this task. We can learn a great deal from them. But the truth is, most of us engage in theology from time to time and it's more a matter of committing to the conversation than possessing specific knowledge.

This illustration may help you start to think about theological conversation. Recall the last time you went for a walk with friends. Now, contrast that with the last parade you saw. What were the differences? Parades have a leader, someone setting the beat and pace. Marching in a parade involves keeping in step. In a walk with friends the pace varies; there will be times of laughter and shouting; there will be times of gentle sharing and quiet reflection; some will walk faster, some slower, so there will be times when the group pauses to let someone catch up, or tie up a lace, or remove a stone.

For most of us, theology is more like going on a walk than marching in a parade. We progress at different speeds at different times. Sometimes we need to pause to assimilate what we've learned. Just like a walk, you can do the work in this book on your own, but you may find it more rewarding and pleasant in the company of others.

Doing theology means exploring our faith. As T. S. Eliot suggests, we may well return, over and over again, to the same questions. There's a very good reason why religious discussions strike us as being circular! But each time we do, we will see those questions in a new light, because we are different. Experience and learning have shaped and changed us—consciously or not. Imagine a spiral (our faith journey) and through the midst of it a straight line (a particular issue or life questions). As we come to different points on the spiral we encounter the same question but we do so from different perspectives and angles. So it is an exploration—a journey where the precise destination may not be clear. We may consult various guides along the way, but ultimately the journey is ours.

This book is about words for faith and some people wonder about the necessity for those. They speak of faith being shown in actions. Well and good—I would never suggest that we substitute "talking the talk" for "walking the walk." But it isn't that simple. From time to time we may be asked why we're acting in certain ways. Sometimes we may want to offer some insight or aid to a friend who is struggling. Even before that, though, the work of putting our faith into words helps us grow and recognize how we have been impacted.

Theology is also necessary because the gospel comes to us in the way it does. After all, Jesus did not speak about international terrorism or global warming or identity theft. But even more to the point, despite the efforts of some to misuse it as a rule book, Jesus did not leave us one of those—so we have to figure out his meaning in relation to the struggles and triumphs, the joys and sorrows of our own everyday living. Most of us who call ourselves people of faith or Jesus-followers are doing that anyway—when we do it consciously it's theology.

Theology is necessary because of what the community of faith is. If your community is anything like mine, it is a long way from a group of likeminded and identical robots! Instead, we are a fellowship of unique and precious individuals, originating in different places, of different chronological age, drawn to various facets of the tasks which Jesus left us. Most of us, at some level, want to be true to his call. But true living is neither thoughtless nor careless. Theology can jolt us awake and stir us from familiar patterns, increasing our awareness of what we have done and left undone.

Theology is conversation. Conversations take many forms with many people. The conversation may have pauses (perplexed, anxious, puzzled). Unlike a speech which continues towards a pre-determined end with a pre-established set of words, conversation often involves waiting—for God, for our conversation partners, and even for ourselves. That's why there is so much emphasis in this book about telling stories. Our words about God arise from stories—the stories in the bible, the stories of our community, the stories of the world around us, your story, and my story. Instead of taking one story and making it the only story or the *normative* story we want to gather many different particles into a new whole that we can own. A theological story is about God and people. What does it look like? Let me suggest some examples:

- a child asks "did God make a caterpillar just like God made me?"
- a teenager storms out of the house shouting "Don't talk about God loving me when you don't!"
- someone asks, "how can I believe in a just and loving God when I see starvation in Africa, brutal violence in the Middle East, and persecution in so many places?"

Whether they know it or not, all those people are doing theology. They are asking theological questions and offering theological observations in word and deed. One way in which we do theology is as we live our faith, acting alone or in company with others—questioning, answering, acting.

Here's a second way we do theology:

- a church group struggles with the decision to paint the church nursery or give to missions;
- a worship team wrestles over several meetings about appropriate language for prayers and hymns;
- a group of congregations meeting together, debates with great heat, acting to protest the opening of a quarry that some say will threaten the local water table;
- a national body tries to respond to a report advocating boycott of products produced in the occupied West Bank by Israeli-owned companies.

These are official bodies of the church. Every denomination has them by different names. They have responsibilities and often seek to balance scripture, reason, tradition and experience in a deliberate way as they seek to reach answers.[1] This is a second way of doing theology—as responsible groups work at, question and seek to sort out, a theological position that leads to actions for the whole community of faith.

Here's a third set of examples

- a theologian sits at her desk struggling to condense and summarize 2,000 years of Christian practice around baptism into guidance for you and me;

- a national committee of twelve people try to work out a policy for the church on the challenging question of physician-assisted dying;

- the national decision-making body reads, discusses, and finally adopts new liturgical resources for congregational use.

These are people, often labelled experts, undertaking theology on behalf of the rest of us. They are employing specialized gifts, interest and training to look back into our past practices, analyze our current situation, and challenge us with new understandings of faith. It's important to remember that while this is often what comes to mind when *theology* is mentioned, it is far from the only way in which we share words about God.

EXERCISE #1—THE FAITH LIFE LINE

One of the simplest places to begin doing theology is with our own lives. It may be the story that we know best. Telling the story in the way suggested here invites us to pay attention to where we may have encountered God and not been aware of it. On a piece of paper draw a horizontal line. Now, divide the line into equal sections of five or ten years. List the significant highs or lows you

1. Those four terms are often referred to as the "Wesleyan Quadrilateral" which we'll explore in a few pages.

experienced at that time. Remember, this is your life line so you determine what is significant. Here's a random fictional example.

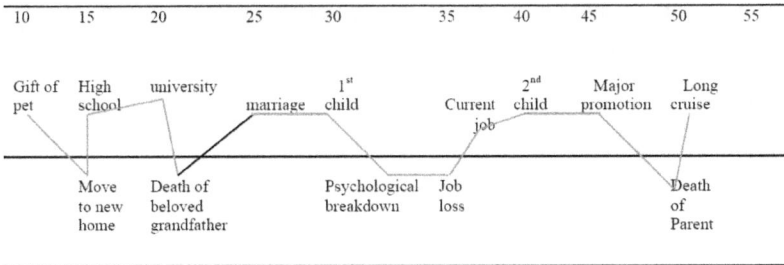

10	15	20	25	30	35	40	45	50	55

Gift of pet | High school | university | | marriage | 1st child | | Current job | 2nd child | Major promotion | Long cruise

Move to new home | Death of beloved grandfather | | | Psychological breakdown | Job loss | | | | Death of Parent

This individual has had the sort of life journey that many can identify with—emotional highs and lows. Depending on the person, some of those could have been reversed. They recall the move to a new home as negative, but high school was a good time in their life. In another person's life, those events could spark a reverse response. So, after you have noted the various highs and lows of your life journey take a few moments and ask yourself: "Why do those events have those associations for me?" "What— very specifically—makes them high or low?" "Who was present that helped or hindered me at those times?"

When you recall those events in detail do you remember any sense that more was going on than you can fully account for? That more could take many different forms. Perhaps there was a feeling of safety or security in a difficult time that had no logical basis but, nonetheless, was quite real. Or maybe one of those people you identified showed up at just the right moment for no discernible reason. Could it be that, in the intervening years, you've grown into an awareness that, in the midst of terribly difficult circumstances, there were gifts that you didn't perceive at the time? Did you survive an event in a fashion for which there was no logical explanation—people may even have called it a miracle?

Those can all be indicators of the presence of the Divine. Many people associate God's presence with what insurance contracts call "acts of God": essentially events for which no other explanation is possible! While those do occur, the greater truth

For many people this can be a very emotionally challenging exercise. It may call to mind a multitude of different feelings that you may want to share with your pilgrimage companion(s) or someone you trust.

Can you identify a time when you felt the undefinable presence that you had faith was holy?

How did you know what you knew? What were the feelings, sensations, awareness?

Have you ever shared that experience with anyone? Can you try doing that? What hopes or concerns would you have in sharing?

is that the Holy often works in and through people and processes which seem altogether normal and natural. Except there is often a little *something else*. The person who appears as they are needed; the resource that comes available at just the right time; the strength that we find when we thought we were finished; the insight that we gain, either instantly or over a span of time, that recasts our experience in a new light. To the attitude of faith those can be evidence of the Holy. Recall that we defined faith as, "trust or confidence in something or someone." That's what these may be for you—not evidence to withstand scientific testing but truth that is deep, real, and life-changing.

EXERCISE #2—THE WINDMILL

Once we have become aware that God has been present in our past experiences, we may become interested in learning to discern that presence in our current events. There are tools for that and they can be used by individuals or groups. The underlying conviction is that *God is present and active in our lives and the life of Creation.* However, discerning that presence and developing a faithful response is not always easy or quick. Sometimes a tool or instrument can help us break down an overwhelming question into its constituent parts, making it easier to process.

There are many models for this process. Here we will explore a couple of the more concrete. The first is *The Windmill.* Why a windmill? One of the ways in which the Jewish and Christian traditions refer to God is as *breath* or *wind.* The wind is always blowing but we rarely see it directly. More commonly we see the results of its passage in the movement of trees and flags and so on. A windmill depends on that breath for its action and the wind is always blowing. So too, our thinking about God in the world is going on all the time—whether we realize it or not. In those moments when we stop and become intentional about our thinking, we move into *theological reflection.*

The other thing about a windmill is that it can catch the breeze on any blade. So too, our thinking about God can start at

17

any point. So, any point in this windmill can start us thinking. As we revolve we move toward the centre—a moment of insight. The movement of the blade creates new energy and we decide how to use it.

Consider the four blades of the windmill. Remember that none is more important than or primary to the others. So, we can consider them in any order. Let's consider the story with which I started this chapter, media reports of terrorist attacks.

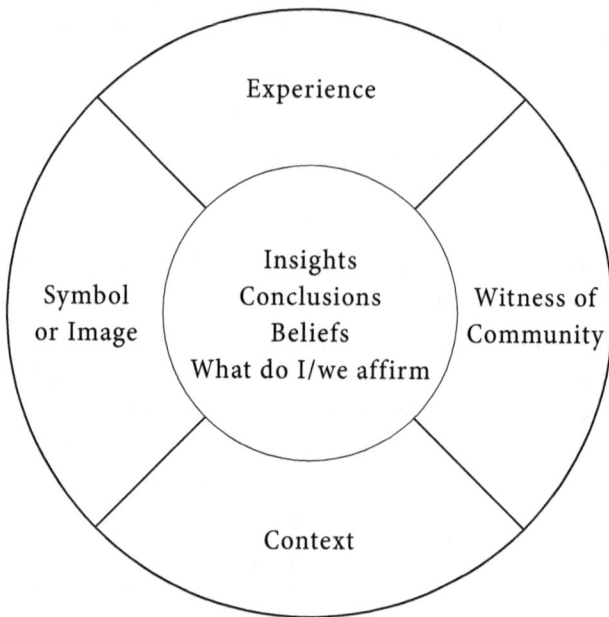

The blade of *Experience* invites us to describe the event and the feelings it inspires. We need to gather everything we can that factors into our response. This includes not merely the objective data: location, numbers of dead and wounded, level of disruption, and so on, but also the feelings, thoughts and assumptions that the experience inspires. Perhaps we are caught up in the horror of such an event or, alternatively, we have become numbed to them. We may instinctively feel the "wrongness" of such acts or we may perceive them as a legitimate response to actions in other countries. We may be conscious of certain images in our mind of suicide bombers and those may link to our assumptions about immigrants in general. These are just some of the aspects of *experience* that we might have and it is important to be clear about them as we reflect.

If we turn to a *Symbol/Image* we are tapping into our creative impulses to develop a symbol or image or dream that the focus of our reflection inspires in us. We are bombarded by many photographic images of news events, but we are creative beyond what is fed to us. The same news event might inspire a sense of grim darkness, a phoenix of hope rising from the ashes of destruction, a biblical image of weapons being converted to tools of nurture, a dream of reconciliation between differing parties, and so on. Once again, there is no one right image, but in calling to awareness the image/symbol that touches us we are exploring another aspect of our spiritual insight.

A further blade in the windmill is *Community*. Most of us are part of some sort of community—indeed we may be part of several. It may be an organized community of faith, or a political party, or an ethnic group, or a social gathering. Since our reflecting in this case is theological, an obvious community is one of faith. That may be as structured as a religious community (church, synagogue, mosque, etc.) or something more informal such as a study group or prayer group. The more structured it is and the longer it has existed the more likely it is that the *community* has formed opinions on subjects. It may have a series of sacred stories that inform outlook on life events. There may be a shared sense of God's vision for the world and/or words of judgment and promise. When we turn to the *Community* blade of the windmill we acknowledge that we do not stand alone but that there are other resources available to us. It may be that our honest answer is: "I don't know what my community says/thinks/believes about certain life events." In which case, this blade is encouragement and motivation to dig in and find out. Because this is a windmill, the assumption is that discovering your community's stance on a specific event (assuming it has one) will not end the process of reflecting but continue to add to it.

The fourth blade is *Context.* We all exist within a context that has implications for our views of the world, our relations with other people, and the judgments we make of world events. Often those things which seem obvious to us are that way only because of the context in which we live. Used in this way *context* is neither good or ill—but if we are to reflect honestly, we need to bring to consciousness the truth of who we are. The fact that I am a white, middle aged, upper middle class, educated, articulate, professional, heterosexual male brings with it certain advantages and disadvantages. It affects the way I view the world and, unless I am aware of it, I may assume that everyone thinks the way I do, or that my view is the correct view, or that God endorses my view of the world. None of those make for particularly honest reflection! So here are some elements you might consider in becoming aware of your context:

- Our place in the power structure of life. Which of the following best describes your social position? When you think of the life you live daily, would you consider yourself: outsider; oppressed; a woman, a man or member of a minority gender group; part of a racialized minority; part of other minority groups; a child; an authority figure; part of the dominant or controlling group; or something else;

- Our place in the social structures of life. If we are fully employed, marginally employed, under-or unemployed it will impact our context. Similarly, the sorts of work we do and whether they are fulfilling or not.

- Our place in family or other constellations of support will impact our context;

- The values and ideologies we hold will affect our context. Are you essentially individualistic or communal in your outlook? Do you believe that, in the end, might makes right or do you hold a different view? Do you have particularly strong feelings about capitalism or other economic systems and those who do not succeed in those terms?

Having done all that we are now able to say not only what we believe or affirm, but, far more importantly, why I or we do so. That gives us a foundation to stand on when we dare to answer the question: "where is God?" (which will loom even more important in the next chapter). We began the process searching for meaning in a given situation. The result is an experience of empowerment: instead of being confused and despairing we have a new insight which leads to a sense of energy. What will we do with the new energy?

EXERCISE #3—REFLECTING ON CURRENT EVENTS

If you experience a gap when it comes to applying your faith to events you see going on around you daily or you encounter in the media—relax, you're not alone! For many people, instead of their faith assisting them it seems to remain silent. This increases a gap they may feel between the faith they celebrate on Sunday and "real life" Monday to Saturday. Or perhaps, when a preacher or writer unpacks the faith/spiritual component of a public issue they see the connection but they struggle to do that on their own. Again, the disconnect is reinforced. For some people the disconnect becomes so pronounced that they give up faith community entirely (one of many reasons people leave).

In this exercise, we want to look at some randomly chosen statements about world or community events that may test our faith. It's important to note that they are not meant to preference the positions of any church or spiritual tradition, nor do they assume that there's a right answer we should adopt. They're meant to give a focus for the next step of our journey.

Step One is to answer them quickly—just circle the answer that feels right. *Please note:* if you're doing this as a group exercise *do not* ask what people answered. No one is expected to share their results although I do encourage you to talk about how the process felt after you finished. If you don't have an answer, go with your inclination.

SOME BIG QUESTIONS

The death penalty is moral and necessary in some cases	YES	NO
We have a national responsibility to intervene in international situations of injustice	YES	NO
Our spiritual commitments require us to adopt a simpler lifestyle with a smaller ecological footprint	YES	NO
Properly regulated doctor-assisted dying is consistent with my faith tradition	YES	NO
International terrorists correctly represent the teachings of their faith	YES	NO

After you have answered these questions choose the one that was easiest or most straightforward for you. Thinking about your response to that question answer the following:

- What is the crisis—or decision-point for me? (Or, what is the bottom line?)

- As I understand God, what is God's nature and purpose? (Or what is God's wish for humanity/creation?) How does my understanding of God relate to this question?

- If I had to sum up the teachings of Jesus (or another spiritual teacher that I deeply admire) what would I say? How does that answer relate to this question?

- Do I have any personal experience with this issue? Are there times when I have acted or spoken on this subject (or didn't when I could have)? What happened? What have I learned from all that experience?

- Does my faith community (locally or nationally) teach anything on this subject? If I don't know where could I go for answers?

- In the light of all this—how might I think/act/behave as a person on faith?

How did you feel about that? Was it tough to do? Probably. It should be. If it felt artificial I sympathize. However, if you've ever learned a musical instrument or other art form, or mastered a physical discipline, you may remember how that felt artificial in the beginning. Anything that has been practiced for centuries has certain steps that have developed over time known for being the best or most helpful. Most of us weren't born knowing how to ski, or play jazz piano, or drive a car. It takes learning and practice until it becomes second nature. So too with theological reflection. But if you followed through with the process you might be in a new place: a place where you can state why, as a follower of a faith, you believe or act as you do. You've been doing theological reflection. You've been reflecting on God (*theos*) and putting those thoughts into words (*logos*) about God, the bible or the community of faith. Congratulations! It's a big step. Now, when you feel ready, go back through the process again with the big question you found hardest to answer.

EXERCISE #4—MOVING FROM REFLECTION TO ACTION

If you've worked through the last exercise, then you are ready to move on to the next stage. One of the greatest challenges for many North American people who feel committed to specific faith traditions or spiritual practices is how to translate our good ideas into good actions. We may have all these wonderful, faithful ideas about the world but then we come face-to-face with our lives as they are and we wonder, "How in the world can I act on those ideas?" or "How can one person, or a small group, make any difference?" So, our faith becomes a very private thing and a so-called Christian nation ends up looking just the same as it would without the "Christian" part! By the example of huge (and sometimes very costly) change, our sisters and brothers in Latin America and Africa have reminded us of the importance of faith issuing in action. To put it bluntly: all the right thinking in the world will not change anything without action! The following model is designed to help you go from thought to action.

As well as being good for individuals, this model works well with a group. Consider the chart you see below. There are three columns and five rows. The columns are about actions and the rows are about the various factors which influence our thinking/doing. It is particularly oriented to those who identify themselves as Christian, but it can be used by those who identify with other traditions or no specific tradition at all.

GIVENS	ACT OF WILL OR EXERCISE OF CHOICE	HOW
The situation we face is part of real life	Face up to the question or issue (Cease denial)	By analyzing the situation and asking "what is really true here?"
Our faith heritage in relation to this issue or question	Claim your tradition. What is good or bad in how your faith has traditionally related to this question?	By looking at scripture and our faith tradition
Thought and action	What will I think about this question? What will I do about this question	By combining thought and actin. Recognize that we can't know everything and can't do everything—but what will we do?
Experience and insight	Learn from them. What do I know from previous encounters with this issue?	By honestly reviewing our experience
Past/Present/Future	Trust	When we recall the presence of God in all of our times then we trust that we can learn and grow

Interpreting the chart

The first line asks us to face up to the real life situation by analyzing it to the best of our ability. For example, you might be wanting to reflect on the apparent absence of younger people in your community of faith. As you face up to the real situation you may need to gather data about where young people are actually found. One possible result is that there are young people—just not where you expect them to be. Another possible result is that your impressions about your congregation being largely composed of an older demographic are accurate. In either case, it is important that we base our reflection on accurate data.

The second line invites us to claim our Christian heritage. Suppose we shift the focus of inquiry to *international terrorism,* we might inquire as to our heritage in relation to the Middle East and Moslems. We should also explore whether our faith community has any contemporary statements about Moslem-Christian relations (many denominations do).

Line three is the movement to action. How will you better understand or remedy the situation? Maybe the plan is to canvass the young people you can identify to clarify their needs and wishes. Or maybe you want to open a dialogue with a nearby mosque. How will you do that and what steps are needed? In line four we seek to learn from our experiences: what do we know now that we didn't know before? have new questions been raised? how can we continue to move forward with our issue or concern?

Line five is terribly important: in all that we do, whether as individuals or as groups it is important to remember both who we are and whose we are because we bear the name of Jesus Christ. Now, try it yourself. Identify an issue with which you feel some familiarity and about which you want to know some facts (maybe it's one of the big questions from Exercise #3). Run through the various stages. See what the results are. Have some fun!

The Wesley Quadrilateral

In the last thirty years, many books on discernment and decision-making, have employed something called "The Wesley (or Wesleyan) Quadrilateral". It arises from the thinking and writing of John Wesley, the founder of the Methodist movement that arose in the Church of England in the 1700s, and which has a long lineage with many different names, in Protestant Churches around the world. The Quadrilateral was first explained in detail by a Methodist historical scholar, Albert Outler.[2] He discovered in Wesley's sermons and theological writings a "method" or decision—making that identified four components: scripture; tradition; reason; and experience.

REASON	TRADITION
SCRIPTURE	EXPERIENCE

Here's how it might be employed when looking at a particular portion of the bible:

Experience:

1. What experience was this passage originally for or about?

2. What did this passage mean to and for the first readers?

3. Is the experience written about timely (meant specifically for the original audience but not applicable today) or timeless (has meaning for all readers of any time)?

4. How is this passage similar or different from your own experience of God?

2. For example, see his edited text of Wesley's writings, Outler, John Wesley, iv.

Reason:

1. What might have been the thought processes of the original writer?

2. How does this logic inform your own ways of thinking?

Scripture:

1. How is this passage similar or different than other passages of Scripture you have read before?

2. Is this passage based on another passage of Scripture? If so, what was the original context for the other Scripture passage?

Tradition:

1. What traditions (Jewish, pagan, philosophical, etc.) did this passage of Scripture come out of?

2. What traditions is it speaking to?

3. What do others (i.e., commentators, other people, etc.) say about this passage?

4. How does this passage affirm or conflict with the traditions in your church or family?

In some denominations (for example the United Methodist Church)[3] the Quadrilateral played an important role in discussion about controversial subjects such as leadership roles for women in the church, homosexuality, and same-sex marriage. The argument was generally made that, while biblical passages that spoke clearly on those subjects were often identified, they ran counter to the reason and experience of God's people and an overall scriptural message of empowerment. Without for a moment disputing the conclusions that were reached it seems fairly clear that Wesley would have challenged the way the Quadrilateral was employed as a representation of his method.

While the model is helpful for reflecting on events in our life or in the world there are a couple of notes of caution. The first is that

---

3. *The Book of Discipline of The United Methodist Church*, 76—83.

it is drawn out of John Wesley's writings—there is no evidence at all that he ever developed it or employed it himself. More significantly, as it is usually pictured the four quadrants are equal in weight and importance. This would not be the case for Wesley himself: *scripture* would have an overwhelming and dominant role in his thinking. Finally, when Wesley referred to *experience* he generally meant it in terms of the sort of results we developed at the end of Exercise #1. For him, it was not simply any experience of a particular event in our lives, but experience as understood in the light of faith.[4]

What experiences have you had talking about current events or big questions from a spiritual or faith perspective?

How did that go? Did you feel adequately equipped for the conversation? Why? Why not?

After completing this chapter do you feel any more able or confident? What do you need to do next?

4. It's worth noting that, later in his career, Albert Outler specifically rejected the term "Wesley Quadrilateral" as being employed in ways that he did not intend.

Chapter 2

You the Story Teller

A friend of mine recently purchased the franchise for "MoMonday" in our city.[1] The concept is quite simple: everyone has a story to tell and enough people are looking for a venue in which to tell it and enough people are willing to pay to listen and support the telling that you can make a business of it! And it works. There are MoMonday events in a variety of Canadian cities (thirteen as I am writing this chapter). Last evening, at their opening night, I

---

1. See http://www.momondays.com. Accessed March 31, 2016.

listened to six "ordinary people" tell their stories. By ordinary I mean, not professional speakers or clergy or lecturers or politicians, or presenters. They weren't selling anything (that's against the rules) or pitching causes or dogmas (that's not allowed either). Rather they gave ten minute accounts of either specific, life-altering events or how significant moments changed the arc of their lives. There was laughter, and tears, and moments of that profound sort of silence which, to me, indicates that we are on holy ground. There was a depth of honesty that I have rarely heard in faith communities. So, while I considered it a great privilege to attend to these vignettes of real life, a part of me was wondering about the nature of our society that creates such a desire that allows storytelling to be a viable business. I have nothing against business and I am very grateful that folk have stepped forward in different communities to foster this safe (and indeed holy) space. But I still have the question: why aren't we doing this in faith communities? And if we wanted to do that, what are some tools that would further that? One of the aspects of MoMonday is that the speakers receive help and coaching in framing their story. That's the purpose of this chapter: providing some tools to draw out and help give shape to the story God is writing in your life.

For most of human history *story* has been the primary vehicle for the transmission of wisdom. Whether we consider great spiritual texts, foundational myths of Greeks, Romans or Norse communities, the teachings of First Nations elders—the list is seemingly endless of the importance of stories in shaping communities. That's true in our own experience: one of the ways we know we have arrived and truly belong is when we know the foundational stories of a specific group. Much of the fascination with genealogical research lies in knowing the stories of forbears. In knowing those stories, we come to know ourselves and our current place.

However, in many parts of our society story has a diminished or weakened status. We may recall our parents or grandparents asking, "are you telling me a story?" when they doubted the truth of our words. We may contrast *story* with *fact*, granting to the latter a reliability that we deny the former. In popular speech *myth* is often synonymous with untrue or superstitious and we treat the myths of societies as the primitive stories of unlearned people trying to cope with what we ("accurately") explain by means of science. Thus, for many decades, certain parts of the Christian community have tried to place the myths of the earliest parts of the Abrahamic story shared commonly by Jews, Christians, and Moslems on a par with science. In so doing, accounts intended for one purpose are shoehorned into a role they were never intended to play. Both detractors and promoters of those accounts as fact miss the fundamental reality grasped by some cultures: *truth* comes in varying forms and can be accessed in a variety of ways. Thus, a story can be profoundly true without necessarily having to be—or even claiming to be—factually accurate. Until the dawning of the scientific method and its adoption in many fields, cultures could quite happily accept multiple and differing accounts of the same event, not insisting on choosing one as *right* but recognizing that the fullness of *truth* could sometimes only be approached through differing accounts. Examples abound: the two creation accounts in Genesis; the two accounts of the life and reign of King David; the existence of four gospels; the earliest forms of written history (right up through the 1600s) where differing accounts lay side by side in the same text.

So, as we begin to explore your role as story teller—particularly in relation to the deep things of life—it may be helpful to recognize that *truth* and *factual accuracy* are not necessarily synonymous. No, I'm not suggesting that you lie about your past! I feel confident in saying that lying and telling the truth are fairly clear opposites! But it's not necessary to remember all the details of an event—or even to recall them as others do. This is particularly the case when we tell our stories of the actions of the Holy in our lives. That may well be a very personal perception that is simply not accessible to anyone else. That doesn't make it wrong! We need to trust our stories—but not necessarily absolutely.

Consider the following diagram of the three elements of story and truth. The premise is that what we call *truth* is not held by any one part but arises in the intersection of stories.

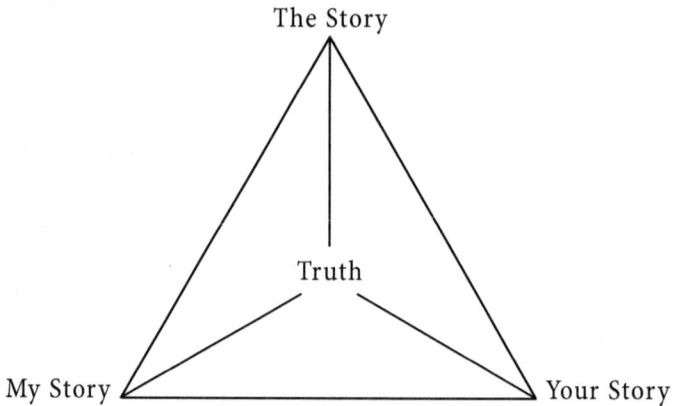

The Story

Truth

My Story   Your Story

The Story in this model refers to whatever overarching account we give authority to. For Jews that might be *Torah,* for Moslems, the *Koran,* for Christians the *Bible,* for Hindus the *Gitas,* and so on. However, depending on your fundamental spiritual and faith commitments, you might well choose other accounts. For some libertarians it is the writings of Ayn Rand; for neo-Nazis it might be *Mein Kampf;* for some it might be Nelson Mandela's, *Long Walk to Freedom.* For still other people *The Story* may not be found in a written text but comprises the teachings of the elders. I am not trying to ascribe any moral equivalency or worth to those sources! My point is simply that, for each of us, there is an overarching story that we employ to make sense of the world and which impacts how we interact with others. Thus, for Christians, the bible is a record of human interaction with the Divine in history, primarily in the people of Israel, in Jesus of Nazareth, and in the early communities of Christ followers. It is celebrated in worship, word and sacrament and used as a basis for ordering life.

My Story in this context refers to the reality we began to understand with the exercises in the previous chapter. What does my life line reveal about my journey and particularly the interplay with the Holy during that journey? Faith journeys, like stories, are to be celebrated. There are no two alike. Do we dare to believe that our stories are an important part of the unfolding of *The Story?* In Christian terms, is our journey genuinely a portion of God's unfolding relationship?

Your Story is the other person with whom we are in contact. Unless we are simply telling our stories to ourselves (which may have considerable merit in some circumstances), they are the person with whom we are sharing our story. They may be a person of faith or not; they may practice a specific spirituality, or not. My invitation is that, in telling our story, we treat them as individuals of worth and—whether they are aware of it or not—someone with a faith story. Where they are, where they come from, is the result of a combination of choice and circumstances. That helps create their stories, which we must respect.

TELLING YOUR STORY

So, how will you go about telling your story? If you are already comfortable with this, you may want to skip this section. It contains a few ideas to help beginners.

- Storytelling is interactive. The story itself emerges from the cooperative and interactive relationship of speaker and listener(s);

- Storytelling presents a story. In other words, listing out a set of facts is not a story. They need to be woven together in a narrative

- In storytelling, the listener imagines the event, often without any other resources than the words being used (no pictures, audio track, movies and so on). So, the storyteller needs to share important aspects so the listener can enter the account[2]

- Storytelling takes different forms in different cultures. It can also be employed for many different purposes. In this context,

2. See the Story-telling Network, "What is Story-Telling," http://www.storynet.org/resources/whatisstorytelling.html, accessed April 1, 2016.

I assume that we tell one another stories so that we can comprehend and celebrate the place of the Holy in our lives. The only thing we are seeking to convince another person of is our conviction that there is more to life than what is visible on the surface

- Storytelling weaves information and emotion. You not only want to tell someone about something but you want them to feel it as well. Generally, we want them to share the feelings we had during the experience

- Essentially a story expresses how and why life changes. It is about how, in the midst of the seeming ordinariness of our daily routine, something surprising occurred that created change. It is something that throws life out of balance. It could be a major crisis or simply a new awareness. The story goes on to tell how we seek to bring life back into a new form of balance. A storyteller should aim to help us feel what it was like to deal with opposing forces, or dig deeper, or stretch our minds, make difficult decisions and ultimately discover the truth

- For beginning storytellers, it is important to remember that your listener does not have all the facts until you share them. They don't know what time of day it was, how you were feeling, where you were, whether you were hot, cold, calm, nervous, happy, elated, scared, grieving, and so on. They may not recognize the significance of the event until you tell them why it is important. For instance, if I simply say, "That day I missed my bus," my listener can sympathize but it's not very involving. However, if I say, "On the day I went for that important job interview, I missed my bus," then I've immediately raised the stakes in the story

- Finally, help me to care about your story. If I care about the story, then I will gladly continue to listen to you. The best way the help me care about the story is for you to care about it. If you don't care about what you're telling me, then why should I?

EXERCISE #5—STORY TELLING

Now we're ready to try some story telling. Relax and have fun with it!

#5a. For the first exercise think about an event that occurred in your life in the last 24 hours. It doesn't have to be dramatic, in fact every day and ordinary might be more helpful at this point. If you're just getting started in this activity, it may help to jot some notes:

1. Picture the setting in your mind and try and recall the various physical elements: location (where were you?); time of day; temperature (were you hot or cold?); smells and sounds (natural or mechanical sounds, conversation, radio, video, etc.); furniture or physical features (grass, trees, leaves, rocks, water); and people (who was there, what did they look/sound like, were they friends or strangers?)

2. How were you feeling as the event began? Bored, excited, restless, calm, happy, sad, frightened, excited, tired, rested?

3. Why were you there—wherever the event took place. Was it on purpose or by coincidence? Was it a familiar space or someplace new for you?

4. What happened? What words were spoken or actions taken?

5. How did you feel during and after the event? (see the list at b). What was the result of the event? What did it mean to you?

In most stories, you would not include a fraction of those details, so don't be overwhelmed! But when we get into the habit of paying attention to details then we'll be more involved in our stories and more involving for our listeners. We'll draw them in! For the person of faith, the encounter with the Holy is found in incarnation—in places, people and things that are real. We rarely if ever encounter the Divine in abstraction.

#5b. For our second exercise, take the details you compiled for #5a and frame a brief story. Choose only those elements that you need to convey why this event is meaningful. Tell it to one of your pilgrimage companions. Invite them to respond, clearly and specifically, to those elements of your story that worked best for them and to suggest places where you might have altered, added or removed, material.

#5c. Go back to Exercise 1 in the previous chapter and choose a specific event that you'd like to be able to talk to others about. Work through the various stages in #5a above to develop the elements of your story. Then, add another stage: why does this event have spiritual significance for you? Help me to understand what there is in the elements you've identified or in addition to them, that gives it that significance. Then repeat exercise #5b with this event and tell a faith story.

What were your responses to the various stages of story-telling?

What aspects of story-telling were the easiest; the most challenging; or surprised you?

What were your feelings as you told these stories?

Did you feel differently telling the faith story? If so, how? How would it have been different to tell that story to a comparative stranger?

EXERCISE #6—SHARING OUR FAITH STORIES WITH OTHERS

One of the major challenges in sharing faith stories with others arises when we fail to understand that this is a journey that all people take individually. Until we talk about it, it is quite natural to assume that the faith experience and journey of other people are the same as our own. Once we set aside the assumption that there is one route to faith we can begin to open ourselves to the wonder and diversity of people and their journeys with God. Who knows what we might learn!

The following model works especially well for those who claim a faith or spiritual stance; and orient themselves generally within the Christian tradition. It may also be helpful for folk who identify themselves differently. Here are a couple of important things to keep in mind.

- this model is designed to help us understand the diversity of faith journeying. It is not intended as a template into which we shoehorn personal experiences—our own or others';
- this is primarily oriented towards Christianity. It would be quite wrong to apply this as if one tradition has universal applicability, although the similarities may surprise us;
- not everyone has experienced what they call faith. Respectful hearing allows them to name their experience in their own way. In the next chapter, we will explore ways of faith story

sharing with those who experience (and name their experiences) the world differently.

Begin by exploring the "rooms" in this house of faith. Which rooms have you experienced in your life up to now? Are you aware of having moved through more than one? Can you recall specific events that characterized each room for you? Are there rooms with which you are personally unfamiliar? Where are you dwelling spiritually right now? If you have pilgrimage companions take the opportunity to share this aspect of your faith journey, remembering that there is no one right path. Take your time.

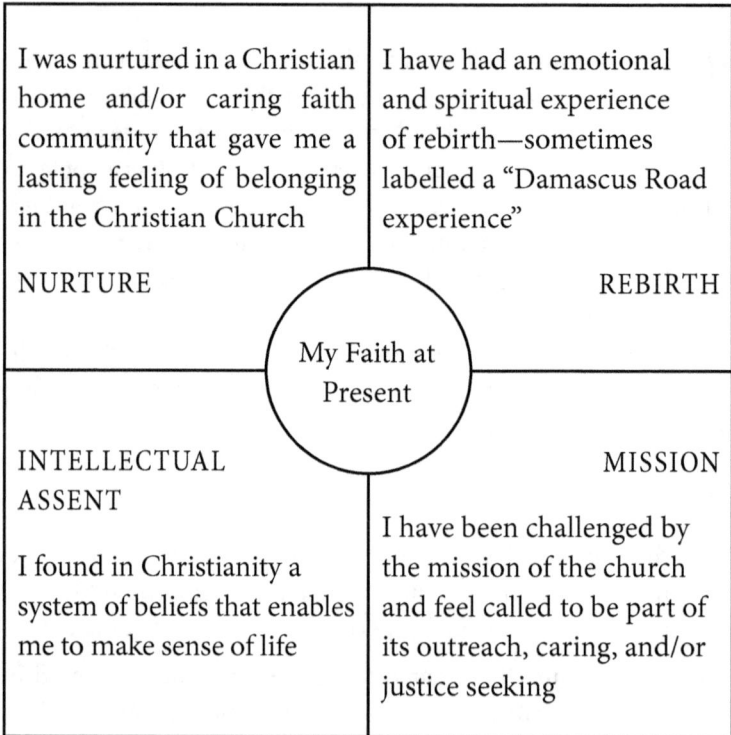

I was nurtured in a Christian home and/or caring faith community that gave me a lasting feeling of belonging in the Christian Church NURTURE	I have had an emotional and spiritual experience of rebirth—sometimes labelled a "Damascus Road experience" REBIRTH
INTELLECTUAL ASSENT I found in Christianity a system of beliefs that enables me to make sense of life	MISSION I have been challenged by the mission of the church and feel called to be part of its outreach, caring, and/or justice seeking

My Faith at Present

What did you learn from the rooms of faith exercise about yourself and your companions?

What were the "aha" moments for you?

Do you feel the need to rethink your attitude towards anyone in particular on the basis of these new insights?

Chapter 3

You the Faith Sharer

We are simply asked
to make gentle a bruised world
to tame its savageness;
to be compassionate of all (including oneself);
then in the time left over
to repeat the ancient tale
and go the way
of God's foolish ones.

(written by an anonymous Jesuit)

As I walked the streets of New York City on Good Friday, I was struck by by the thought—is this what it was like in Jerusalem so long ago? In most other places I've been, Good Friday is a statutory holiday and the atmosphere is radically different—especially downtown. In New York that day, it was just like any other. Manhattan's sidewalks were crammed with people, the sounds of a dozen different languages and dialects falling on my ears. The streets themselves were filled with fleets of urgent, honking, pressing traffic. There was some sort of security alert that led to a noticeable increase in armed soldiers at the intersections (perhaps like Jerusalem on that tense Passover weekend). All of these folks were going about their lives, living out their story and—in different places here and there—some of those who called themselves Jesus-Followers were gathering to remember. In Little Italy, we stumbled across the end of a community Stations of the Cross parade, with a couple of hundred parishioners from two or three parishes following a group of costumed folk to the "tomb" in the middle of an elementary school play yard. Police (off-duty? on overtime? supplied by the city?) were providing traffic control as these folks told a portion of their faith story in word and song and the narrative of an ancient, cruel and ever-relevant event. I overheard a young mother trying to explain to her daughter what it was all about, this story being played out which was, apparently, just on the edge of her knowledge.

W hen we come to share our stories with others—particularly those who are outside our normal circles of faith and spiritual practice—we need to think about *why*. Why do you want to tell someone else story and, as part of it, why faith is important in your life? Lots of possible reasons come to mind. What are yours?

Unfortunately, faith sharing is often caught up in recruitment. Sometimes it's called *evangelism*. That term makes many uncomfortable because it has become associated with certain techniques, activities, and goals that we cannot endorse. Which is unfortunate because the term evangelism simply means, "sharing good news". In Christian terms, "the Good News" (often called the gospel) is the story of the impact God in Jesus has had on us and on the whole Creation. The problem is, *evangelism* has become associated in popular thinking with a specific outcome: the person being evangelized is supposed to agree to certain things, respond in certain ways, and undertake certain actions (often joining a specific faith community). While those may sometimes be laudable in themselves I believe we need to decouple sharing the good news of what the Holy means in our lives from anything that follows.

Can you think of a time when you shared your faith with someone or shared the account of an event where faith played an important role?

What were the circumstances? What moved you to share your story at that time? What was the result and how did it leave you feeling?

Conversation can be one of the richest gifts of human experience. Two people, genuinely sharing what is important to them. One speaks and then the other. There is silence, laughter, tears, verbal and non-verbal connection. And always—*always*—the possibility that we might be changed in the encounter. For many people, sharing faith stories carries a peculiar set of burdens. Partially, I think, because we confuse that with religious conversation. I can't count the number of people who have said to me, "What if they ask me something I can't answer?" Suppose you were talking with a friend about a movie or book that particularly touched you, and they asked you a question you couldn't answer. What would you do? How would you respond? Does knowing that could occur prevent you from speaking about those topics? That's why I have been stressing that these are *faith* conversations, not *religious*. By saying that, I hope to relieve you of the sense that you must be either an authority or a defender of religion in general, a specific tradition, or of precise details. That's not your job!

Sometimes, when faith conversations occur, someone will raise the various dark and troubling aspects of religious history. Often the speaker may not grasp that those events are even more troubling to those inside the faith tradition! But it doesn't have to be a conversation-stopper if we remember that we are sharing faith not defending religion. The simplest answer is the honest one: "Yes, those things trouble me too. I try to balance them with all the good that has been done. And honestly, they don't affect my faith experience directly." Your experience gives integrity to your faith. It is the reason for you to believe—not for proving to anyone else that what you believe is true, but why you believe it. If your conversation partner recounts an occasion of personal injury at the hands of religious folks or institution, what do you do? The same thing you would do if they told a similar story about anyplace else or any other group. Don't defend, empathize. "That is truly awful. I'm sorry that happened. It has left a mark hasn't it?" And if someone should ask you a question of *fact* that you can't answer—what a fabulous opportunity for you both to continue the conversation! The best response is: "I don't know, but let's find out together." Trying to bluff our way through situations where we don't know is unfair and dishonest. A faith journey that is ongoing is far more attractive to others than one that pretends to have arrived. Why should you be expected to be an expert on everything related to your tradition? I expect that my family physician will have certain core competencies, and know when she is beyond her expertise and refer me to someone with more specialized knowledge. I don't think less of her for not knowing every detail of this wonderfully complex creation we call the human body. Knowing enough to say, "I don't know but let's find out together," is a sign of genuine maturity.

MODERN	POST-MODERN	LIBERAL	ORTHODOX
"Don't tell us fairy tales"*	"Tell me a story"	"I don't want to interfere or impose my story on you"	These are the objective spiritual truths to which we must agree
Prove it! Reality is expressed best in evidence	Emotionally driven & aesthetically responsive	"Truth" is subjective—it must be evaluated and owned individually	There is a truth beyond subjectivity (and often research)
Comfortable with individualism and consumerism	Hungry for affiliation and belonging	Don't want to intrude; tolerant; open to new learning	The individual decision is central to salvation
What is the individual's relationship to gospel?	Curiosity about and openness to community in the life of faith	Express and embrace tolerance and diversity to certain limits	Holy writings reveal truth of what is needed
Preference for "facts" and "propositions:	Truth is in the relationship	Non-judgmental about truth—yours and mine	There is an "objective truth" that is greater than individuals
Prefer rational, definable, verifiable, materialistic accounts	Reject pressure to stand in a particular position or believe a specific way	Respectful of science and truth as a concept—unsure of the possibility of knowing	Truth is God-given. Our task is to discover and accept it
Evangelism is superstitious non-rational thinking	Ambivalent about evangelism	Evangelism difficult if it begins by saying something is wrong with the other	Salvation in a particular way is real and necessary
Evangelism = sales	Expect a buffet of spiritual choices	Can be "evangelical" about evangelism's evils	Conversion is crucial

*For instance, many religious studies courses in the 1960s and 1970s gave "natural explanations" for biblical miracles

EXERCISE #7—UNDERSTANDING RESPONSES TO FAITH STORIES

Recalling the household of faith exercise #6 you may remember that we saw there are several ways in which the Holy interacts and connects with human lives. One the one hand, people are unique—wonderfully, creatively, chaotically, often confusingly different. On the other hand, there are some similarities which may help you think about the friend or neighbour with whom you might share your faith story. Consider the preceding table. It shows four different—very broad—ways in which people might approach spiritual and faith stories. These are broad characteristics and very few people fit only one column. Chances are that people will be a mixture of modern/postmodern with liberal/orthodox. But please don't try and force people to conform to the chart. Use it to clarify your insight.[1]

Consider the characteristics in the table. Where would you place yourself? Are you modern or postmodern? Are you liberal or orthodox? How have those qualities expressed themselves in your faith journey so far? If you are undertaking this book with others compare your results.

Consider someone you know well and think about where they fit in this table? What experiences of them lead you to that conclusion? Based on that, how would you need to shape a faith story in order than they could hear it? Do you think they'd be open to hearing your thoughts about faith in your life? Why or why not?

FURTHER THOUGHTS ABOUT CHALLENGES

Let's face it: for many people anything that hints of "evangelism" raises discomfort and confusion. Part of the problem is that many well-known forms of evangelism have been experienced as manipulative and disrespectful. They are associated with arguments that seem essentially directed towards "not going to hell." It's hard

---

1. Developed from materials present by Dr Robert Fennell in a presentation entitled, "Evangelism in a Postmodern Liberal Mainline Christian Denomination: Four Paradoxes and Tensions", delivered, 4 Nov 2014. Used with permission

for me to accept that that's what Jesus was talking about. He spoke of the kingdom of God, something that was "in the midst of you" or "within your grasp".[2] It's not surprising that people in faith traditions—particularly but not exclusively Christian—are leery of reoffending. In our *religious family* stories there are lots of instances where people have been colonized—spiritually, economically, politically, geographically—and exploited in the name of faith. We have profound motivation to not repeat that!

Increasingly the people you encounter with whom you might share faith stories will fall into the category of post-modern in the chart above. It's not necessarily a matter of age as it is one of experience and outlook. Most of us are so bombarded with advertising and political messages and various causes shouting for our attention that we have become, as a matter of self-preservation, cynical, and skeptical. Anyone age fifty or over has lived through the apparent failure of science and technology to solve all society's problems. When we are told that something is "bigger", "faster", "better" we are doubtful. If your conversation partner is a post-modern that is all to your advantage. For post-moderns anything presented with a four-step program and diagrams is immediately suspect because they feel intuitively that the truth comes in far less packaged ways. It comes as poetry and art. It is a story and discovered in the interaction of people. It comes less as "something I have that you need to have too," than as "this is how I see the world, what do you see?" So, we are less likely to offend the other person if we are not claiming to have something they need but merely sharing the wonder of our common pilgrimage in life. Like you, I have had the experience of someone telling me why I needed to have exactly what they had—and were often trying to sell me! It's boring, tiresome, and sometimes offensive. I have never been offended when someone told me that something was important to them and why. I may not have felt the need for whatever it was in my life, but I wasn't offended by hearing their story.

2. Luke 17:20 The Greek phrase is entos humon which has sometimes been mistakenly translated "within you", encouraging a concentration on the individual spiritual life and a split between the inner and outer person.

STORYTELLING MOMENTS

One of the challenges with discredited forms of evangelism is that they seem to impose their agenda on whatever is happening in someone's life at that moment. So, for example, someone knocks on your door and, totally oblivious to and seemingly uncaring about what is happening for you, wants to talk to you about "Jesus." The evident message is that they have something that you need so badly that it transcends all other concerns. Clearly that is not what I am advocating!

Instead I am inviting us to a process of paying attention to what others say, looking for those moments where we might be invited into another's life. Those are points where we are invited to come into another's life and, if we are open to it, recognize the opportunity to share our story. This is not a solution to whatever they are confronting but an opportunity to remind a fellow human being—you are not alone. That feeling of being alone may be one of the most devastating experience we humans can have, and all the great faith traditions have important responses to that common dilemma.

EXERCISE #8—ENTERING THE CONVERSATION

It's interesting how most of us are born able to talk, but not necessarily communicate meaningfully. Similarly, most of us can hear, but do not as a matter of course know how to listen. Listening is demanding—I can tell if I've been listening because when the conversation is over I'm tired. Alternatively, if I'm not tired after an encounter I know I wasn't fully attentive. Here's what I mean: as a rough rule of thumb active listening involves me talking *less than 20% of the time.* For some people, listening 80% of the time is going to be hard work. Some professions spend years learning to listen but there are some basic communication skills which are so helpful in faith story sharing.[3] In previous exercises we've looked

---

3. A quick Google search will take you to many sites—some of them free— where you can explore and enhance the very basic skills introduced here. If

at how to tell a story. To complete the package, we'll consider how listen to a story. This will require you to work with at least one other person. If you've had training in listening skills, you may want to skip this exercise.

Consider this poem:

> To sit where they sit
> To stand where they stand
> To hear what they hear
> To see as they see
> To be who they want to be
> To touch the edge of another's life
> To heal the pain of the world's need
> This is being the Christian Story.[4]

What does this say to you about listening? Have you ever experienced being listened to in that fashion? What was that experience like? A basic conviction is that the other person is worth listening to. Are there some people who you think are not worth your time? Better get clear on that now!

Basic skill #1 — "I" language

"I language" takes ownership of our feelings and our responses. It does not lay blame on others. For instance, it does not say, "You make me so angry"; it says "When I see you do that, I get very angry." It does not ascribe feelings or motives to others. For instance, "You did that because you hate me." Instead, "When you do that, I feel like it shows hatred. Is that true?" "I language" is a very powerful tool for accurate communication. and very helpful in understanding what the other person genuinely means.

---

you're interested, I strongly encourage you to pursue this as something which will enhance every aspect of your relationships.

4. Turner, Being the Christian Story, 77.

Basic Skill #2—The Paraphrase

When we respond to the content in another's story we need to take seriously *what* they are saying before we move on to *why*. There are several phrases that we can use. It's not a matter of memorizing these but of understanding the purpose and achieving that. Examples: "you're telling me that"; "am I hearing you correctly that"; "You are saying"; "I think that I heard you say."

With your pilgrimage partner: Partner One tell a story about something that happened this week. Partner Two, listen and then use one or more of the questions to test out your reception of the details. Then reverse roles.

Easy, right?! But terribly important, so that we start with correct information or we can go very wrong.

Basic Skill #3—The Perception Check

The feelings and emotions behind the words are of great importance when we're sharing faith stories. If we genuinely want to hear the other we need to be attuned to their voice, their facial movements, their body language, and so on. Those are the hidden communication elements that constitute 80% of the content. It's also a place where it's easy for us, as listeners, to go astray. We make guesses and assumptions about the meaning of the material for the other person. But we can be wrong. Have you ever had the experience of hearing something and having a reaction totally different than the speaker's? So, we test out our perceptions to make sure we are getting an accurate read. This is not about assigning a value judgment. Examples: "I sense you are feeling"; "It seems you are afraid of"; "I get the feeling that"; or, "Is it possible that you might be feeling."

With your pilgrimage partner: Partner One tell a story about something that happened this week that had some emotional content for you. Try to avoid stating directly what you felt: "It was great" or "I was angry." Partner Two, listen and then use one or more of the questions to test out your reception of the feelings. Then reverse roles.

Basic Skill #4—Open Ended Questions

These are questions that ask for minimal information to clarify something that has already be shared. When we are receiving someone's faith story we are on holy, and perhaps tender, ground. We want to avoid any impression that we are criticizing or interrogating the other. But we may need more information to make sure we fully understand the content of their story. So these are non-threatening and non-probing questions that build only *on what the other person has already offered.* They do not make a demand to go any deeper than they have already shown willingness to go. Examples: "I'm not clear about what you said when you mentioned . . . "; or "Can you help me understand what you meant by . . . "; or, "Help me to better understand . . . "

With your pilgrimage partner: Partner One describe a hobby or activity. Partner Two, use any of the basic skills to clarity information. Then reverse roles.

CONGRATULATIONS! You are now a better communicator than 80% of the population. You have begun to develop the skills that can make you a significant gift and blessing to others! There are a multitude of other skills that we can develop in the repertoire of active listening but these certainly get us started.

EXERCISE #9—PRACTICING THE CONVERSATION

Before you move into faith stories you might want to practice your newfound skills on important conversations that might arise in your work, school, community or social situations.

In collaboration with your pilgrimage partner, choose roles ("story teller" and "active listener") and role play the following scenarios. Remember to use the skills you've learned.

#1 You're talking to your friend about your spouse, whom you are angry at because he/she is consumed with work, is always at the office, and has missed several important outings with you and the family. You're feeling somewhat embarrassed and don't really want to "air your laundry" in public, but, at the same time you feel a real need to talk about it.

#2 You're talking to your co-worker. You are very excited because you are planning your first vacation in five years. You leave next week. The only thing that you worry about is the cost, because money has been tight recently.

#3 You're thinking about quitting your job. You and your spouse have talked about this for a while. It would mean selling your house and moving away to live somewhere less expensive. You think you want to do this but at the same time you wonder if it is the best thing for you and your spouse. You are talking to your co-worker. Take it from there!

Take a few minutes to reflect on the skills you've been learning.

How did it feel to listen in this way? What was the same or different about this in comparison to your normal patterns of listening?

How did it feel to be listened to in this way? Are you used to someone being that attentive to you?

What emotions did it spark in response?

UNDERSTANDING STORY THEMES

When we begin to listen deeply to the faith stories we may find them provoking questions and responses in us. That's a good thing! It seems that many people are seeking places where they can be heard and accepted for who they are at a profound level (more about that in the next chapter). So, it may be helpful for you to think about your response to concerns you may encounter. In researching this book, I asked a group of people to ask some folk they know some very basic questions about what troubled them or gave them joy. These were deliberately a wide range of demographic characteristics (age, gender, economics, education, involved or not in faith community, etc.). I didn't intend for this to be scientific or conclusive in any way. I just wanted something more for you to chew on than just my thoughts. I asked my volunteer researchers to ask their contacts three questions: #1 What breaks your heart?

#2 What do you think breaks God's heart? #3 Who are the poor in our community? The answers might blow you away!

What breaks your heart?

- Child soldiers (15-year-old male, not church involved)

- Suffering . . . Sadness . . . without getting into a therapy session, watching my son when he is upset when he feels pushed away by his mother and seeing this young man in tears. (Male, 53, non-church goer)

- My kids in pain breaks my heart (Male, 40 plus, regular church attender)

- Parents who do not care about their kids. (Male, 19, church goer)

- Mental illness and our poor system for handling it. The pain within our aboriginal communities. Hungry and neglected children. (Woman, 55, regular church attender)

- Giant things like world hunger and child soldiers, and lesser things like watching families crumble . . . Hardship makes my heart break. (Female, 18–20, occasional church attender)

- Lost hope breaks my heart . . . when family members or friends seem to have lost hope because of circumstances like repeated disappointments from others or in themselves. Watching someone on the verge of giving up on life. [W] hen hope is lost by people or communities in the world. When people give up because they have been so oppressed, so tortured, so deflated by their environments it crushes my heart . . . I work to shift my heart from Breaking DOWN to breaking OPEN. Both hurt, but the latter allows room for the light to enter in and for hope to find a way. (Woman, 40 plus, regular church attender)

- Seeing senseless harm inflicted on people or animals (~65, female, church involved)

What breaks God's heart?

- Hurting others breaks God's heart. (Male, 40 plus, regular church attender)

- Perhaps if I had that answer I would be far wiser than I am. . . . senseless hate and anger and death we . . . put on ourselves, or each other, and this planet in the disguise of "peace". (Male, 53, non church goer)

- Bigots, racists and homophobes. I believe God doesn't condone anyone judging another person (Male, 19, church goer)

- I feel God's heart is breaking with the wars, poverty, starvation, injustice, lack of tolerance for those who are different, and my own lack of action on some fronts. I am sure God is wondering what is going to become of her children much the same as any parent wonders. Our world is suffering on so many fronts some days it is hard to find a bright spot. (50 something, female, church goer)

- Anytime we struggle He weeps. Whether it's mentally, physically, financially; openly or privately. God sees and knows all. And His heart breaks when we are not okay. (Female, 18—20, occasional church attender)

- Corporate greed. (15-year-old male, not church involved)

- I don't know that God has a heart in the way that I do. [Perhaps God's heart is] Unbreakable—so flooded with Love that there is room for nothing else and so, it is an endless source of grace waiting for us to receive. Maybe that's why our hearts break—so that God's heart can enter in. . . . (Woman, 40 plus, regular church attender)

- Seeing His children suffer (~65, female, church involved)

Who are the poor?

- The poor are those who are not loved. I think those who do not feel they are loved have to be the poorest of all . . . if you are not feeling loved then all the money in the world will not help. (50-something, female, church goer)

- . . . my thoughts go to those with no hope. Perhaps that is no hope for a home, or a job or a partner or family or recovery. (Male, 53, non church-goer)

- Those who cannot follow their passion for one reason or another. (Male, 19, church goer)

- Those without effective support systems. The lonely. Those who feel unloved and unlovable.

- (Woman, 55, regular church attender)

- The poor embody a wide spectrum. I think of the man who frequents my bus wearing the same clothes every day. I also think about the people in my life who are lost and broken. I take it in both senses. There a lot more poor people than just homeless folks. (Female, 18–20, occasional church attender)

- Poor in the community are those who have lost the true purpose of love in being human in their lives. (Male, 40 plus, regular church attender)

- The poor are those that live in scarcity. [M]any wealthy people . . live in scarcity and although they have money, I would say that their lives are poor as in "that's a poor way to live". [P]eople of lower incomes who lead rich and fulfilling lives focused on the abundance on their lives. Someone with money may be very unhappy and on the edge of death. (Woman, 40 plus, regular church attender)

- I feel the poor are those who locally and globally have not found a place for any religion in their lives. Funny enough however I know people who are spiritual—believe in readings and speaking to others on "the other side"—but God nor church is ever mentioned. In fact, one comment was "I never got into the church thing"—so if the parents think like this then their children don't know any different. (Woman, 60, regular church attender)

- Those without a place to call "home". (15—year old male not church involved)

- Those who do not have a relationship with God. (~65, female, church involved)

What a rich mine of human story! I wish I could talk to each of those folks about their responses! The thing is, these responses come from people just like you and me. They're on the same bus, in the same club, in the same office or school room or community group. As I read the responses I got the feeling that they were desperately eager for someone to listen to their story. Maybe someone like you.

Chapter 4

You the Faith-Sharing Community

"Memories are the key. Not to the past but to the future."[1] *"Healing is impossible in loneliness; it is the opposite of loneliness. Conviviality is healing. To be healed we must come with all the other creatures to the feast of Creation."*[2] *"We speak not only to tell other people what we think, but to tell ourselves what we think. Speech*

1. Ten Boom, *Hiding Place,* 87.
2. Berry, "The Body and the Earth," 99.

is a part of thought."[3]

When people were asked *"what breaks your heart?"* a significant number of them referred to the reality that their children and
grandchildren are not part of the faith in which they were raised—
or any other organized spiritual community. Part of the response
revolved around a sense of guilt that somehow the centrality of
the community had not been adequately conveyed and that adult
children were missing out on significant life-resources. Part of the
concern was that, by not participating, the next generation(s) are
evidencing a self-centredness that ignores the needs for prayer, love,
and support. Part of the concern was that they would not have ac-
cess to those resources in their own times of need. Some are engaged
in *"guerilla grand-parenting,"* as they seek to inculcate something
of the practices of the church despite the apparent indifference of
the middle generation. Often, however, this was counter-balanced
by clear sense that the next generation are involved in the community and active in supporting others—but not from a religious
basis. Which may or may not raise the distinctions between faith,
spirituality, and religion noted earlier.

We are bombarded by the news that the church is dying.
This is generally based on the analysis of data. We are also conscious of the profoundly negative rhetoric that exists around the
church. For many, "judgmental" and "hypocritical" are the initial
responses when asked about the church. The numbers of participating people has been declining for some time.[4] In the face of that
contextual reality some people will latch onto faith story sharing as another technique for recruitment. That can be motivated
by fear: "I am a Christian and if you become one then I'll feel
less like part of a dying breed." It can be motivated by despera-
tion: "We need more people (read: time, energy and money) to
carry the burden." After more than thirty years of congregational
ministry I've seen both of those approaches crash and burn more

3. Sachs, *Seeing Voices*, 85.

4. This is not a new phenomenon. Statistics indicate that, in Canada, several formerly mainline denominations ceased to grow in the mid—1960s. It
just took a while for us to catch on!

times than I can count. Personally, I now realize that I have often confused making church members with making disciples of Jesus Christ. The latter should be our focus not the former. If the church as we have inherited it passes away that will be reason for grief certainly.[5] *But the community of Jesus Christ will persist.*

One of the statistical anomalies of our day is that, while participation in organized religious traditions (of nearly every form) is declining, there are constant signs of deep hunger for meaningful community where people can be known as individuals rather than merely as consumers or employees or statistics. That is part of a wider trend towards more local expressions of community: farmers' markets, community organizations, community banks, neighbourhood food pantries, local festivals and so on. Faith communities can strengthen their local communities by paying attention to issues of education, homelessness, racism, justice, loneliness, and health in their neighbourhoods. Clearly that is not the whole story: there are some issues which must still be addressed on a regional, national and global scale. The challenge for faith communities—particularly those that have been absorbed by concerns for their own survival—is that instead of being drawn up in our own concerns, issues and comfort, we must turn outwards and risk giving ourselves away in the cultivating of disciples of Jesus and not members of the church.

A further challenge of this time is that no one size program fits all. When I began in congregational leadership it was quite simple and straightforward to pick a book or a program on the shelf, change a few words, and lay it down on the congregation. And it would work! There was an apparent broad applicability of program materials across different contexts. If that was true then, it certainly isn't now. Those faith communities that are thriving are the ones that are prepared to risk trying new things in their setting, not because there is a program or outline for it but, because they have prayerfully

5. Few people realize the degree to which the structure of the church which we inherited is a product of various social, economic, and political factors which have very little to do with the basics of the faith.

listened in their community for the Spirit's voice. That's tough stuff and scares as much as it inspires because it includes the possibility of error. And an anxious church—and the church today in most places is profoundly anxious—fears mistakes! The pilgrim church will often travel in uncertainty and bewilderment, as if in the falling of twilight or the false light or early dawn. To quote the early sage: "Sing alleluia and keep on walking."[6] The reality is that, as we contemplate different faith communities, those that are thriving are remarkable in their dissimilarity. Here are some commonalities, however, that relate to the sharing of faith stories:

- Authentic community—a place where people can move beyond the polite chitchat of post-worship coffee hour to real engagement with one another and life's joys and hurts;

- Real sharing—the opportunity to get to know the person who sits, worships, sings, and serves beside you;

- Connecting people to meaning rather than activity—listening to the deep needs of individuals to make a difference in the world rather than filling slots in an organizational chart;

- Focusing outward rather than inward—expending the majority of our resources in serving the world rather than ourselves and taking whatever we have to the world rather than inviting the world to come into our circle.

Faith story sharing is the work of every generation and of every member of the faith community. It is a spiritual practice based on the assumption of a deinstitutionalized approach—namely that there are no *experts* and *supporters* but all have a role because everyone has relationships. It is based in the assumption that God is already present and active before the church gets there. So, an important spiritual discipline is waking up each day with your senses attuned and your life ready to respond to whatever God is up to. That includes listening to stories and telling your own story. Because in the telling and the listening we recognize how our own lives have

6. Augustine, Sermon 256, 1191—93.

been transformed.[7] In those principles there is much to guide our worship, education, mission and justice activities! This will not be universally popular. As Jacob Armstrong observes, "Every church has a Back to Egypt committee" living the lie that claims it was all better back then.[8] The truth is, for many in faith communities today, this is a change of the rules of the game. They signed on with a clear understanding of what a faithful religious life looked like and the place of the church in society. The change of circumstances requires of them adaptive skills that they do not possess and may see no reason for acquiring. For example, one gentleman I know resolutely denies the appropriateness of either sharing his faith story or listening to those of others. It is an invasion of his privacy, his personal relationship to the Divine, and entirely inappropriate in the context of church. His sense of individuality trumps the call to community. The solution is to continue to love them but not allow them to set the agenda. In the words of Brene Brown: "If you're not in the arena with the rest of us I'm not interested in your feedback".[9]

EXERCISE #10—BUILDING COMMUNITY FAITH SHARING

In many congregations there will be groups of pilgrims who will eagerly gather to pursue the exercises in this book and continue to build their confidence and faith. There are a lot of small group resources out there for use. Many resources do a wonderful job of providing us with new information. That is valuable. But we can hide from personal interaction by constantly questing for new knowledge and holding the conversation at arm's length. The key question in evaluating any groups resources is this: does it encourage openness to the experience of God in life and the sharing of those events?

However, folk who are unwilling to venture into a small group—perhaps the majority in established congregations—can

---

7. Gortner, *Transforming Evangelism,* 23 and *Relational Evangelism Project.*

8. Armstrong, *Adopters,* 52.

9. Brown, *Daring Greatly,* 91.

still be helped to become more comfortable and more attuned to the Holy in their lives and surroundings. Here are some possibilities:

- every time a group, committee, choir, board meets, take a few minutes to simply ask the question, "where do you see God active in our community?" and listen to the responses of those willing to share;

- when a choir or worship team chooses or practices hymns, look at the words and talk about what they are saying about life, God, community, people, hope, grace or whatever the topic is;

- encourage existing groups to meet over food or refreshments and get to know one another as people—preferably in a setting they don't normally use;

- when some people have developed skills in story-listening find a place in the community or at a community event where you can be and folk can listen to their neighbours;

- gather a group who are interested in practicing the theological reflection skills outlined here, have them focus on the daily news, and encourage them to share their insights with the congregation;

- explore ways of sharing faith stories through community or social media;

- undertake physical pilgrimages to organizations or institutions that are making a difference and afterward talk about where you saw God in that place;

- Invite any group that is willing to undertake the following story telling using the pattern that is appropriate to their lives:

  - A 1—My life before coming to faith

  - A 2—How I came to faith

  - A 3—My life since coming to faith

  - B 1—The early influences on my faith life

  - B 2—How I made faith my own

  - B 3—My faith life today

- invite a group to reflect on—from a faith sharing point of view—or plan a sermon series on the following:

  □ Spirituality in the mainstream media—what are the spiritual values or faith commitments being shown in news and public affairs; why are certain stories chosen over others?

  □ What does Sabbath mean in the 21st century?

  □ What does community look like in an individualistic society?

I was raised in a society that no longer exists. In that world the assumption was that, if you didn't declare yourself to be something else, everyone was Christian. The job of a church was to make you "our flavour" of participant. Christian rhetoric and symbolism seemed to undergird the whole community so there was no felt need for training in sharing faith stories. Assuming that world existed as more than a dominant class fable, it no longer does. In many jurisdictions it is entirely safe and proper to identify one's religious affiliation as none. *Many different world views and value systems compete for our loyalty. In that marketplace of ideas, those who treasure a specific story and a specific shaping identity as markers on the pilgrimage to truth have a responsibility to share those. Most spiritual traditions—and Christianity especially—are centred on the concept that faith is not simply for my own good. It is a gift and heritage in which I participate for the greater good of those around me and the entire Creation. That's the greatest pilgrimage of all.*

Bibliography

Armstrong, Jacob. *The New Adopters*, New York: Abingdon, 2015.

Augustine. Sermon 256 in *Patrologia Latina*, J.P. Migne, (trans.ed),. Paris, 1863

Berry, Wendell. "The Body and the Earth," in *The Art of the Commonplace: Agrarian Essays*, Washington D.C: Counterpoint, 2002.

Brown, Brene. *Daring Greatly: How the Courage to Be Vulnerable Transforms the Way We Live*, New York: Gotham Books, 2012.

Buechner, Frederick. *Listening to Your Life: Daily Meditations, with Frederick Buechner*, San Francisco: Harper Collins, 1992.

Gortner, David. *Transforming Evangelism*, New York: Church Publishing, 2008

Outler, Albert. *John Wesley*, Oxford: Oxford University Press. 1964

Sachs, Oliver. *Seeing voices: a journey into the land of the deaf*, Berkley: University of California Press, 1989.

Ten Boom, Corrie. *The Hiding Place*, Washington Depot, Chosen Books, 1971.

Turner, Gordon Bruce. *Being the Christian Story*, Toronto: United Church of Canada, 1982.

United Methodist Church. *The Book of Discipline of The United Methodist Church*, Nashville: The United Methodist Publishing House, 2008.